HEROES OF THE
BOOK OF MORMON

Dedicated to
All children of the latter days

A very sincere thanks to all of the children (and parents) who participated to make this book come to life!

Kadee Allred
Benjamin Anderson
Baylee Barnes
Amberlee Bate
Breanna Bate
Mckenna Bate
Savanna Bate
Taryn Bott
Taylor Bott
Tylor Bott
Tanner Breeze
Bridger
Conner Brown
Christian Brown
Dallas Brown
Anson Call
Brady Call
Carter Call
Tanner Call
Parker Christensen
Strom Clark
Joshua Comer
Britain Covey
Christian Covey
Cole Craft

William Redcliff "Chunky" Crank
Jane Croghan
Austin Engemann
Chandler Eyre
Corbin Folkman
Justin Hymas
Samantha Hymas
Andy Isom
Michelle Isom
Russell Isom
Willie Isom
Camille Jensen
Davis Jensen
Joshua Richard Jensen
Journey Liddiard
Carla Martinez
Linda Martinez
Omar Martinez
Cline J. Mattingly
Chase McCloskey
Rachel McCloskey
Gavin McMullin
Katherine Moulton
Jason Money
Colton Murray

Gage Murray
Jacob Murillo
Braden Patten
Madison Patten
Samuel Parkinson
Kiley Rae Price
Creed Rollins
Makai Rumsey
Isaac Russell
Jessica Russell
Luke Sagers
Paxton Schultz
Haley Snarr
Sibley Snowden
Dexter Tapahe
Dwayne Tapahe
Emmaline Thompson
Malia Tuha
Stevoni Vigil
Dason Walker
Breanna Ware
Luke Ware
Jonas Warner
Alec Winegar

Also, thanks to Shauna Nelson, Margaret Weber, and Vanese Van Wagoner for editorial and art direction.

Published by Covenant Communications, Inc.
American Fork, Utah

Printed in Hong Kong
First Printing: October 2001

04 03 02 01 00 99 98 97   10 9 8 7 6 5 4 3 2 1

ISBN 1-57734-910-5

Library of Congress Cataloging-in-Publication Data

Brown, Tony Sorenson.
    Heroes of the Book of Mormon / Toni Sorenson Brown.
        p. cm.
    Summary: Text and photographs of children in costume present stories
from the Book of Mormon
    ISBN 1-57734-910-5
    1. Book of Mormon stories. [1. Book of Mormon stories.] I.Title

    BX8627.A2 B76 2001
    289.3'22--dc21
                    2001042245

HEROES OF THE
BOOK OF MORMON

TEXT & PHOTOGRAPHY BY

Toni Sorenson Brown

LEHI AND SARIAH

By Small Means the Lord Can Bring About Great Things (1 Nephi 16:29)

The Lord told the prophet Lehi to leave Jerusalem because the people there were wicked. Lehi and his faithful wife, Sariah, and their daughters and sons obeyed the Lord's commandment to leave Jerusalem and flee into the desert wilderness. They left a very comfortable life for one that was difficult—even dangerous. They camped in tents and had to hunt for their food.

Twice, the Lord sent Lehi's sons, Laman, Lemuel, Sam, and Nephi, all the way back to Jerusalem. The first time, He wanted them to get the brass plates so they would have a record of their language, their genealogy, and, most important of all, the scriptures. The second time, the Lord sent them back to Jerusalem to convince Ishmael and his family to join them on their journey. Then Lehi's children could marry Ishmael's children and raise righteous families.

The Lord promised that He would guide Lehi's family to a new home in the Promised Land. Lehi did not know where the Promised Land was, but he knew that the Lord knew. One morning, just outside his tent, Lehi discovered a strange, round object—the Liahona. The Lord gave Lehi this compass to guide them through the wilderness. When Lehi's family was righteous, teachings and directions appeared on the compass. When the family lost faith and were disobedient, the Liahona quit working. After eight long years and many hardships, but many blessings too, the Lord guided Lehi's family to the Promised Land.

Today we also have liahonas to guide us when we are faithful. Prayer, the Holy Ghost, scriptures, patriarchal blessings, and living prophets are some of the liahonas that can guide us to the Lord.

NEPHI

Nevertheless I Went Forth . . . (1 Nephi 4:7)

Nephi wanted to be righteous like his father, Lehi. So Nephi prayed with mighty faith. His prayers were answered, and he was blessed with a strong testimony of his own.

Sometimes the Lord asked Nephi to do very hard things—like slaying Laban to get the brass plates, building a ship, and standing up to his older brothers when they were angry. Nephi's attitude was never, "I don't want to," or "I'll try." Instead, Nephi said, "I will go and do the things which the Lord hath commanded, for I know that the Lord giveth no commandments unto the children of men, save he shall prepare a way for them that they may accomplish the thing which he commandeth them" (1 Nephi 3:7).

Once, Nephi's family was nearly starving. They could not hunt because Nephi's brothers' bows did not work, and Nephi's steel bow broke. His brothers and sisters complained—even the prophet Lehi murmured. Nephi was also very hungry and discouraged, but instead of griping or giving up, he went out and made a new wooden bow. Then Nephi honored his father, Lehi, who was the head of the family, by asking him where he should go to hunt for food. Lehi humbled himself and prayed, and the Lord told him to look at the Liahona. It had directions written on it that told Nephi where he could find food.

After Lehi died, Nephi became the spiritual leader of the family. Laman and Lemuel and others in his family rebelled. They wanted to kill Nephi, so the Lord told him to take the faithful people, and the sacred records, and flee.

This was a sad time for Lehi's family. Nephi wished his family could stay together, but he obeyed the Lord as always and became the founder of the Nephite people.

Like Nephi, we can walk in complete faith, knowing that when the Lord asks us to do something, he will prepare a way for us to do it.

ENOS

Because of Thy Faith (Enos 1:12)

Enos was the son of Jacob, a powerful prophet. His uncle was Nephi, and his grandfather was Lehi. Enos had been taught the gospel of Jesus Christ by his parents.

One day while Enos was hunting in the forest, he began to think about his father's teachings. Enos felt sad about things he had done that were wrong. His soul hungered to be forgiven. So Enos began to pray. He prayed all day. When night came, he kept right on praying until a voice told him him that his sins were forgiven, because he had faith in Jesus Christ.

Enos then prayed for his people, the Nephites. The voice of the Lord came into his mind, telling him, "Whatsoever thing ye shall ask in faith, believing that ye shall receive in the name of Christ, ye shall receive it" (Enos 1:15).

So Enos prayed for his enemies, the Lamanites. They were the nonbelievers who had followed his uncle, Laman. They wanted to destroy the sacred records that Lehi's family brought all the way from Jerusalem. Enos prayed that the records would be kept safe and that the Lamanites would be blessed with the gospel. The Lord promised Enos that the records would be protected, and that one day they would be used to teach the Lamanites the gospel.

Enos spent the rest of his life as a teacher, a prophet, and a keeper of the records. He prayed with his whole soul when he repented. He had complete faith in Jesus Christ.

We can learn from Enos, and know that when we seek the Lord in faith, no matter where we are, we can always find him, even in the forest.

KING BENJAMIN

O How You Ought to Thank Your Heavenly King! (Mosiah 2:19)

Benjamin was a Nephite warrior who fought with the sword of Laban to keep the Nephites free. In peaceful times, Benjamin worked hard to teach his people God's commandments. He dearly loved the people he served. When he became king, Benjamin did not charge heavy taxes, but worked hard to support himself and his family. The Nephites loved King Benjamin.

Three years before he died, King Benjamin called his people together so he could bear his testimony to them and make his son, Mosiah, the next king. He had all the families set up their tents with the doors facing the temple, so that they could listen and learn together. He preached from a tower so people could hear him. He also had his words written so others could read his message.

King Benjamin told the people how an angel had taught him about Jesus Christ. Benjamin said that the way to be happy was to be like Jesus and serve one another. "When ye are in the service of your fellow beings ye are only in the service of your God" (Mosiah 2:17). He told the people to give to the poor and help those in need without judging them.

Benjamin had a special love for children. He told parents to teach their children the gospel, to not let their children fight and quarrel, but to love and serve one another. The Nephites believed their king, and they repented.

Although King Benjamin wrote his sermon for the Nephites, Heavenly Father knew that his message was also important for us today, so he had it included in the Book of Mormon.

ABINADI

Except They Repent and Turn to the Lord (Mosiah 11:21)

The prophet Abinadi was not afraid to bear his testimony to the Nephites. He knew that faith was stronger than fear. Abinadi told their wicked king, Noah, that he and his evil priests were leading the people into sin. This made Noah and his priests furious. They wanted to be told how wonderful they were, not that they were lazy and sinful. They were so angry that they wanted to kill Abinadi, but the Lord helped the prophet escape.

Two years later, Abinadi returned in a disguise. But even though he looked different, his message was the same: if the Nephites did not repent, they would be destroyed. Abinadi was captured, tied up, and brought before King Noah and his priests. Abinadi stood before them in chains, and prophesied with great power of the Savior's birth and life, and of His crucifixion, resurrection, and Atonement.

Wicked King Noah was filled with fear and nearly decided to let Abinadi go free, but his wicked priests convinced Noah that Abinadi should die because he would not deny his testimony. So they tied Abinadi up, whipped him, then burned him at the stake. Even while the flames surrounded him, Abinadi continued to bear a bold and brave testimony.

ALMA THE ELDER

As Often As My People Repent (Mosiah 26:30)

Alma, one of King Noah's wicked priests, believed the prophet Abinadi and begged the king to spare Abinadi's life. Noah grew angry and ordered Alma to be killed, too, but the Lord helped Alma escape. He hid in a thicket of trees near a pool called the Waters of Mormon and taught many people the truths he had learned from Abinadi. Alma baptized hundreds of people.

When King Noah's servants discovered Alma, the Lord warned him to flee with his people into the wilderness. Alma and his people discovered a wonderful land where they lived in peace until one of Noah's evil priests, Amulon, found them and made slaves of them. The people of Alma prayed that the Lord would help them. The Lord heard their prayers, and He gave the people extra strength to bear their heavy burdens.

Later, they escaped to the land of Zarahemla where Mosiah, King Benjamin's son, reigned in righteousness. He welcomed Alma and his people, and appointed Alma as the leader over the Church.

Alma served the Lord all of his days. He taught the same truths that the prophet Abinadi had died for. Alma was just one person, but he listened to the truth and became a powerful missionary and prophet.

ALMA THE YOUNGER

Learn in Thy Youth to Keep the Commandments (Alma 37:35)

Members of the Church in Zarahemla were being persecuted by nonbelieving Lamanites and wicked Nephites. Imagine how Alma felt when he discovered that his own son, Alma the Younger, and four of the sons of King Mosiah were among the cruelest persecutors of all! They wanted to destroy the Church of Jesus Christ.

Alma, the prophet, prayed with mighty faith for his son. His prayers were answered one day as Alma the Younger and the sons of Mosiah were up to no good. An angel, speaking with a voice like thunder, called them to repentance. The power and fear of the Lord struck Alma, and he could not speak or move. His father was joyous because he knew that God's power was at work.

For three days and nights, young Alma's body and spirit suffered great pain and torment as he repented. His family, and members of the Church prayed for his recovery. Alma did recover, and he and the sons of Mosiah were converted. Their hearts and lives were changed.

Alma the Younger became one of the greatest leaders in Book of Mormon history, and one of the greatest missionaries ever! His life teaches us that no matter how serious our sins are, they can be washed clean through repentance and faith in Jesus Christ.

THE SONS OF MOSIAH

Bear with Patience Thine Afflictions,
and I Will Give Unto You Success (Alma 26:27)

Aaron, Ammon, Omner, and Himni, the sons of King Mosiah, could have had great riches and power. But after their conversion, these young men only wanted to be missionaries. They wanted to share the gospel with their enemies, the Lamanites, who were terrifying and dangerous.

The Lord promised their father, King Mosiah, that his missionary sons would be protected. They faced many hardships, and much danger, but many Lamanites who had never even heard the name of Jesus Christ were converted, and came to know and love the Savior just as the sons of Mosiah did.

KING LAMONI

Believest Thou That There Is a God? (Alma 18:24)

King Lamoni had never met anyone like Ammon, the young Nephite prince who wanted to be his servant. One day while Ammon and some of the king's other servants were guarding his sheep, a band of Lamanite robbers came to scatter the sheep and steal them. With the Lord's help, Ammon battled the king's enemies and kept the flock safe.

When King Lamoni heard what Ammon had done, his heart was softened. He listened to Ammon, and believed his message. Then King Lamoni prayed to the Lord and was overcome with the Spirit, and seemed to be dead. After two days and nights the queen sent for Ammon. She explained, "some say that he is not dead, but others say that he is dead and that he stinketh, and that he ought to be placed in the sepulcher; but as for myself, to me he doth not stink" (Alma 19:5).

Ammon told the queen that her husband was not dead, but was under the influence of the Lord's spirit. The next day King Lamoni arose, just like Ammon had promised, and bore his brand-new testimony. He knew Jesus Christ for himself. The queen and the rest of the royal household listened, prayed, and they too fell to the earth—all except Abish, a servant to the queen. Abish had been converted to the gospel years before, but she had been afraid to share her testimony. She ran from house to house, hoping the Lamanites would see the power of God and be converted too.

But when the crowd saw Ammon, a Nephite enemy, lying next to the king and queen and the royal servants, who all appeared to be dead, they were angry. Then Abish took the queen by the hand, and the queen rose and bore her testimony. The queen then took her husband's hand, and he too arose. He taught his people the gospel, and many were converted.

THE ANTI-NEPHI-LEHIES

They Became a Righteous People (Alma 23:7)

Lamoni's brother became the next Lamanite king. His father named him Anti-Nephi-Lehi. He was a very righteous leader. He told his people that because their sins were forgiven, they should never go to war again. His people called themselves the Anti-Nephi-Lehies, and their hearts were filled with faith and love. They made a covenant with the Lord that they would never hurt anyone again, and they buried their weapons of war to prove that their promise was sincere.

The Lamanites who were not converted became fierce enemies to the Anti-Nephi-Lehies. Still, the new converts kept their promise. They would even let their enemies kill them before they would defend themselves or harm anyone. Because of this humble example of love, thousands of other Lamanites were converted. Later, Ammon led the Anti-Nephi-Lehies to safety in the land of Nephi, where they became known as the people of Ammon.

HELAMAN AND THE STRIPLING WARRIORS

Never Had I Seen So Great Courage (Alma 56:45)

The Lamanites and Nephites were fighting more fiercely than ever, and many innocent people were being killed. Some of the Ammonites (who were the Anti-Nephi-Lehies) wondered if they should break the covenant they had made to never fight again. Ammon pleaded with them not to. But what could they do? The Lamanites were winning. Then they realized that their children had not made the same covenant as the parents. Two thousand of their sons asked Helaman, Alma's oldest son, if he would lead them in battle.

Helaman loved these stripling warriors as if they were his own sons. Never had he seen such great faith, for these young men had not been trained as warriors. "They never had fought, yet they did not fear death; and they did think more upon the liberty of their fathers than they did upon their lives; yea, they had been taught by their mothers, that if they did not doubt, God would deliver them" (Alma 56:47).

The fathers of these young men would not arm themselves with weapons, but they bravely crossed enemy borders to carry supplies to their faithful sons. The battles raged and the young men fought with the strength of God. None of those stripling warriors were killed, because they knew that spiritual strength is the most powerful strength of all.

CAPTAIN MORONI

So Long As We Are Faithful (Alma 44:4)

Captain Moroni was a courageous and wise soldier who believed faith and freedom are worth fighting for. He always made sure his soldiers had strong weapons and armor. However, Captain Moroni knew that true strength comes from righteousness. He never started wars, but he fearlessly led the Nephite armies into many battles to defend themselves against the Lamanites.

At this time, Helaman, the son of Alma the Younger, was the Nephite record keeper and prophet. He and Moroni worked together to keep their country free. But many of the people wanted a wicked man named Amalickiah to be king of the Nephites. Captain Moroni knew this would not be good for the people and he "rent his coat; and he took a piece thereof, and wrote upon it—in memory of our God, our religion, and freedom, and our peace, our wives, and our children—and he fastened it upon the end of a pole" (Alma 46:12). Moroni called it the Title of Liberty.

Captain Moroni then went among the people, asking those who were willing to make a covenant of righteousness to come forth. Many people came running to show their loyalty to God and to help Moroni keep their land free. Captain Moroni pursued Amalickiah and his followers until they fled into the land of the Lamanites. Then Captain Moroni "caused the title of liberty to be hoisted upon every tower which was in all the land" (Alma 46:36).

Captain Moroni was so righteous that when Mormon abridged all of the records to make the Book of Mormon, he wrote, " . . . if all men had been, and were, and ever would be, like unto Moroni . . . the devil would never have power over the hearts of the children of men" (Alma 48:17).

SAMUEL THE LAMANITE

If Ye Will Repent (Helaman 13:11)

Samuel was a Lamanite prophet who bore a very special testimony of the Savior. The Lamanites were being converted to the gospel, but the Nephites were living in great wickedness. Samuel told the people of Zarahemla to repent or they would be destroyed. It was the same message Lehi had preached in Jerusalem nearly 600 years earlier.

The Nephites were cruel to Samuel and kicked him out of their city. But the voice of the Lord told him to go back and deliver his message to the people of Zarahemla again. The Nephites would not allow Samuel back into their city, so he climbed up on a wall and began to preach. He told the people that they must repent and believe in Jesus Christ. Samuel also told them that in five years a sign would be given to let them know that Jesus had been born. "Great lights in heaven" would appear the night before Christ's birth, and there would be many other signs and wonders.

Samuel told the people that the sign of the Savior's death would be total darkness and destruction for three days and nights. No stars. No moon. No sun. Mountains and cities would crumble. Thunder, lightning, and earthquakes would change the earth. Only the righteous would be spared.

Some Nephites believed Samuel and asked to be baptized. Others shot arrows and threw stones at him. The Lord protected Samuel, and he escaped. He went to the land of the Lamanites to preach to them and prepare them for the greatest event in the history of the world—the Savior's ministry on earth.

Five years passed, and only the most valiant did not doubt that Samuel's prophecies would come true. They waited, watched, and prayed, but the nonbelievers scoffed. They said the time for Samuel's prophecies had passed, and they set aside a day "that all those who believed in those traditions should be put to death except the sign should come to pass" (3 Nephi 1:9). The new star did appear. A day passed, and when night came there was no darkness. All of the prophecies concerning the Savior's birth were fulfilled.

BEHOLD YOUR LITTLE ONES

∞

Blessed Are Ye Because of Your Faith. And Now Behold,
My Joy Is Full (3 Nephi 17:20)

For three endless days and nights, the darkness was so thick that no light would shine, not even a candle. The destruction was so great that mighty cities were destroyed. The sorrow was so deep that the people mourned with all of their hearts. That is when the voice came. It was the voice of Christ, the Son of God, telling the people that He had been crucified for their sins, and that He loved them and wanted them to believe in Him.

Then after many days had passed, a voice came again. This time it was the voice of Heavenly Father. "And it was not a harsh voice, neither was it a loud voice . . . but it did pierce them to the very soul. . . . Behold my Beloved Son, in whom I am well pleased, in whom I have glorified my name—hear ye him" (3 Nephi 11:3, 7).

The people looked up and "saw a Man descending out of heaven, and he was clothed in a white robe" (3 Nephi 11:8). And when the people heard His words, they were astonished. "Behold, I am Jesus Christ, whom the prophets testified shall come into the world" (3 Nephi 11:10). Lehi, Nephi, Jacob, Enos, Benjamin, Abinadi, Alma the Elder and Alma the Younger, Ammon, Helaman, Samuel, and every other prophet in the Book of Mormon had testified that Jesus Christ would come—now He was here, among the people.

They went to Him. They bowed before Him. They kissed His feet and touched the scars in His hands. They knew Jesus Christ for themselves.

At a special time, Jesus blessed them for their great faith and then He "wept . . . and he took their little children, one by one, and blessed them, and prayed unto the Father for them. And when he had done this he wept again; and he spake unto the multitude, and said unto them: Behold your little ones" (3 Nephi 17:21-23). And the heavens were opened, and angels came down and ministered to those dear children.

Jesus stayed with the people for as long as He could, blessing them and teaching them. Before He left, Jesus called disciples to guide His Church when He was gone. People wrote down what had happened so they would never forget, and so we could have a record of those miraculous times.

After Christ left, all of the people were converted and believed in His teachings. There were two hundred years of peace and prosperity. People remembered what it was like to have Jesus among them. They treated each other with love and kindness.

But in time, a group of people broke away from the Church and called themselves Lamanites, just like when Lehi first brought his family to the Promised Land. Little by little, Satan got into the hearts of the people until Lamanites and Nephites were divided and battling each other again. Pride filled the land. Evil replaced good, and there was no peace. There was no happiness. But there was a righteous record keeper named Mormon.

MORMON AND MORONI

Repent... and Build Up Again My Church (Mormon 3:2)

For more than nine hundred years, the people in the Promised Land—America—had kept written records. Now, it was up to one man to read all of those writings and abridge, them into a single set of records, which were called plates.

Mormon was just ten years old when he was chosen to become the record keeper. He was a good and righteous young man, and when he was fifteen years old, he was visited by the Lord. Mormon was also a mighty warrior and a righteous prophet. As he grew, he watched his people choose evil over good. He led the Nephites in battle, but he was angry and sad when they refused to give God the glory for the battles they won.

The Nephite people refused to listen to Mormon's message about Christ, or to keep His commandments, and the Lamanites overpowered them. Sorrowing over the wickedness of his people, Mormon led them once again in their final battles against the Lamanites, where hundreds of thousands of people were slain.

Mormon knew his enemies would destroy the sacred records he had kept if they found them, so he hid them in a hill. He bore his testimony that these records, the Book of Mormon, would come forth in the future to help convince people that Jesus is their Redeemer. Then he left the records in the safekeeping of his son, Moroni.

After Mormon was killed, Moroni became the only survivor of all the Nephites. He finished writing on the gold plates, which would become the Book of Mormon. The record was then "sealed up, and hid up unto the Lord, that they might not be destroyed" (Title Page, Book of Mormon).

BROTHER OF JARED

What Will Ye That I Should Do? (Ether 2:23)

Jared and his family lived near the tower of Babel during a sinful time. Because the people were wicked, the Lord confused their language so they could not understand each other. A faithful man, who is known in the Book of Mormon as the brother of Jared, prayed that the language of his family and friends would not be confounded. The Lord answered his prayer, and promised to lead those people to a land choice above all other lands, just like Lehi's family.

The Jaredites made preparations to travel to their new land. The Lord showed them how to build barges (round boats) so they could cross the sea to the Promised Land. When the barges were built, the brother of Jared prayed because there was no light or air in them. The Lord told the brother of Jared how to make a hole with a stopper in the top and bottom of each barge so they could get air. But the Lord gave no instructions for light. Instead, He asked, "What will ye that I should do . . . ?"

The brother of Jared made sixteen small, white, clear stones and asked the Lord to touch them. He knew the Lord could make them glow so they would give light in the barges. The Lord touched the stones with His finger, and they glowed. Because the brother of Jared had so much faith, the Lord then showed not only His finger but His whole self to him.

The Lord brought the Jaredites safely across the waters to the Promised Land. For a time, they kept the commandments, but eventually, they became wicked. Then, because they would not repent, they fought until they were completely destroyed off the face of the land. All that remained was the record of a people who chose not to keep the commandments of God.

Moroni understood how tragic the story of the Jaredites was because he had witnessed the complete destruction of his own once-prosperous people. He knew it was his sacred duty to preserve a true record that would convince people to believe in Jesus Christ and keep His commandments so they would not suffer the same fate. Moroni included an invitation to all who read the Book of Mormon to ask God if it is true (Moroni 10:4). Then he buried the gold plates in a hill called Cumorah—the same hiding place his father Mormon had used—and waited until God called him to bring them forth again.

JOSEPH SMITH AND THE ANGEL MORONI

The Heavenly Messenger Delivered Them Up to Me with the Charge That I Should Be Responsible for Them (JSH 1:59)

For hundreds of years, the full and true gospel of Jesus Christ was not on the earth. There were many churches, and they each claimed they were the true church. This was very confusing. Then one spring day in the year 1820, a young, fourteen-year-old boy named Joseph Smith sought a quiet place to pray. He too was confused, but he had read something in the Bible that gave him hope. "If any of you lack wisdom, let him ask of God . . . and it shall be given him. But let him ask in faith . . ." (James 1:5-6). Joseph went into a grove of trees not far from his farmhouse in upstate New York. He knelt down to ask God which church he should join. God the Father and Jesus Christ appeared to young Joseph and told him not to join any of the churches, because none of them had the whole truth. They told Joseph that if he was faithful, he would be the prophet who would restore God's true church to the earth once again.

Three years later, as Joseph knelt in prayer next to his bed, his room grew light. An angel appeared to Joseph—an angel named Moroni. It was the same Moroni who had buried the gold plates hundreds of years earlier. Moroni became Joseph's teacher, and in time, gave the gold plates to the young prophet so he could translate them into the precious, sacred record we know today as the Book of Mormon.